HAROLD COPEMAN

PUBLISHED AT OXFORD BY THE AUTHOR

Published in the United Kingdom
by Harold Copeman

First published 1990

British Library cataloguing in publication data
Copeman, Harold, *1918-*
The Pocket 'Singing in Latin'.
1. Latin. Music I. Title
783.043

ISBN 0-9515798-1-9

Cover and title page by Margaret Farley
after Geofroy Tory's type design (1529)

Typeset from the author's Locoscript 2 discs
by Text & Graphics, Oxford

Book made by Oxford Print Centre

The author's full book ***Singing in Latin*** is available from Harold Copeman, 22 Tawney Street, Oxford OX4 1NJ, at £25/US$40 plus postage.

Or from leading music booksellers.

THE POCKET 'SINGING IN LATIN'

Introduction

This book is for singers and conductors who wish to have with them at rehearsals some short notes about Latin pronunciation. It gives pronunciations appropriate for music in various periods and countries, and specimen phonetic texts from different countries and periods. For those wishing to adhere to the Roman Style it has a brief summary on pages 38–39.

Latin pronunciation is a subject on which strong opinions are voiced. Disagreements sometimes arise through confusion between classical and medieval Latin, and sometimes because people grow up in choirs with different traditions about what is 'right'. I do not attempt here to justify my detailed suggestions, but after a brief account of the background (which may clear up some confusions) I give references to the full data and arguments in my *Singing in Latin*. (Publication details of this hardback book are on the opposite page.)

Whether singers attempt vernacular pronunciations must depend on their skill and on their aim. Singing is combining words and music into one set of sounds, and we may feel that we ought to try to make their styles consistent in the way the composer intended. To do that we need to know something of the manner of performance of the time, and then apply a sympathetic but critical imagination.

But there will be readers who prefer one standard pronunciation throughout their singing. They will be able to use my summary of the Roman style, or of the 'compromise' version of the National Federation of Music Societies (N.F.M.S), in tables D and G below.

In what follows I have avoided footnotes and detailed arguments, though I give a few illustrations of sources. My *Singing in Latin* contains fuller statements; references to these are here abbreviated to *SiL*, followed by page number or by chapter reference.

PART 1: THE BACKGROUND

HOW LATIN DEVELOPED

Two thousand years ago Latin was both a literary language (Classical Latin, pronounced as in schools today) and the less refined day-to-day language of Rome, and of the countries that came under Roman rule. The Western Church worshipped at first in Greek, but later developed a 'Christian Latin' for its liturgy.

The Roman Empire rose and fell: for more than another thousand years classical Latin was preserved, at first by a very few scholars and then, from the Renaissance, by many more. But all the time some form of Latin survived as a living and working language. Christian Latin led to **Medieval Latin**, which was for many centuries - until the new national languages gradually took over - the language of government, diplomacy, law, science, poetry and educated communication. This, not Classical Latin, is the language in which the texts of our music are written.

In the Roman colonies the sound of Latin depended on where one was. Speech took on local accents, especially once the natives came to speak Latin as well as their own languages, Celtic, Germanic and other. (Latin accents in Gaul were notorious.) The local Latin turned into new 'Romance' languages (French, Italian, Spanish, Portuguese, etc.), once it had changed so much as to need new spellings and grammar.

But Latin itself was still in use in those countries for many purposes, including the liturgy and its music: its sounds resembled those in the new languages, but the Latin spellings and grammar were kept. In England and north-west Europe, where the local language came from Germanic invaders, Latin (which was introduced by missionaries) likewise took on a local flavour.

From time to time, starting with Charlemagne, classical reformers tried to remove what they saw as corruption of the language. There were major attempts in the sixteenth century in England and France to return to classical pronunciation, but 'Restored Classical' which they aimed at has only became general in academic use over the last hundred years.

Another reform cut across this. In 1903 Pope Pius X issued his decree *Motu proprio* on reform of church life, and he made it known that he wished Roman (Italianate) Latin to be used universally in the Roman Catholic Church. That Church has now switched nearly completely away from Latin: but many choirs with no allegiance to the Pope still adopt something vaguely resembling 'Roman Style', often with the feeling that this is an ancient usage of the Church. The traditional Latin pronunciations in England and (after great resistance) France have practically died out; in Germany, traditional Latin has been less affected by linguistic changes and reforms, and is still widely used.

But in the last few years a good number of professional and skilled amateur groups have been seeking to bring to English, French, German and Iberian music, as well as to Italian, something of the sound the words had when the music was written; and this book is mainly for them.

CAN WE KNOW HOW LATIN WAS PRONOUNCED?

It is right to be sceptical when assertions are made about the sound-qualities in the centuries before sound-recording: but we should also be wary of received traditions, which may have been distorted and/or reformed.

The evidence about earlier sounds and styles is substantial, though far from complete. I survey it in *SiL*, chapters 5-11; a few samples follow. Chapter 3 applies all the evidence that has so far come to light.

England (*SiL*, ch. 5-9, 11).

Kyrie eleison. The syllables could be simplified: an early carol tells of the goings-on during Mass of the priest and his 'Aleyson', which is rhymed with *Kyrieleyson*; and Skelton, around 1500, has *Kyry*. Playford, around 1650, lists Byrd's 'Kirries'. So the Greek *ie* (ιε) and *ei* (έη) were not treated as double vowels (though *ei* might be sung as a diphthong): it was a change when Byrd moved to *Kyr-i-e* in his two later Masses.

Long or short endings? Classical vowel lengths were no longer strictly observed: *nobīs* classically ended like 'fleece', but now rhymed with 'it ĭs', *virginĭs*: so *nobis* ends in *ĭs*.

E, AE and OE are such common variants of spelling that the *Revised Medieval Word-List* normally disregards them. The usual spelling in manuscripts was E; pronunciation followed that.

S between vowels: a 1528 text says it 'pronounceth by .Z.', but that this was 'corrupte' - i.e. did not conform to classical pronunciation, which reformers were trying to introduce, against massive opposition from the Church. For our purpose we can look for, and perhaps adopt, examples of 'corrupt' usage.

The *GN* sounded like ng-g-n. Around 1400 we have *Angnus*, and around 1500 *magnus* rhymed with 'hange us' and 'strangle us'; both these verbs had a hard 'g', as they have today in some parts of England. In 1580 the traditionalists, 'old customaries', were complaining that reformers omitted the 'ng' sound before the 'g'. By then Latin was not sung in public worship in England, but Byrd was still writing.

France (*SiL*, ch. 10b, 10g, 11b.

In the mid-sixteenth century John Hart put the Lord's Prayer into a phonetic script to show both French and French Latin. *Pater noster qui es in celis, sanctificetur nomen tuum*) became 'pạter noster kiez in selịz, santifisetiur nomen tiuium' (a dot under a vowel indicating lengthening: and see B6 below). Later in the century there was a French fashion for macaronic puns: *omnia*/ Fr. 'on y a', and so on, sometimes indecently.

Central Europe (*SiL*, ch. 10c, 11c, 11e.

Ornithoparcus, as a young church singer from north Germany, travelled around Europe listening to services, and in 1517 wrote his *Micrologus*, which John Dowland later translated. Of one part of Germany, 'I would haue the *Francks* to take heede they pronounce not *u* for *o*, as they are wont, saying *nuster* for *noster*. The countrey Church-men are also to be censured for pronouncing, *Aremus* in stead of *Oremus*'.

To use this kind of data, one has to know something of the phonetic development of English, French, German etc. (Many scholars have worked on this: *SiL* Bibliography, 315-20.) There were waves of reform in the pronunciation of Latin in England and France in the 16th and 20th c., though less so in Germany.

PART 2. SUGGESTED PRONUNCIATION FOR SINGERS

A practical exploration, given a competent choir, will show whether the music and the actual singing gains from using a pronunciation from the composer's time and place. A Bach or Beethoven Mass may sound more convincing with German Latin than with Roman Style; Poulenc will sound quite different in French Latin, and Tallis and Byrd take on a different colouration with Tudor Latin. But in preparing music for performance there are decisions to be made: for instance, in a liturgical service a Roman Catholic choir still using Latin may feel a duty to use the Roman style, especially if it is familiar to clergy and congregation. And in a concert one cannot sensibly chop and change pronunciation during a short group of items, except for a deliberate purpose; it may be better to plan the programme so that these groups are coherent in style and background.

If the composer moved about during his career (Lassus, Schütz and others: *SiL*, ch. 10g) one needs to consider whether to aim to interpret his intentions, or his personal preferences, or to follow the ways of the court or municipality where his music was actually heard at the time. This leads to intriguing argument on various planes - the role of the French and the Dutch/Flemish languages in the southern Netherlands, where so many composers were born; Roman and north Italian speech; the travelling maestro and Netherlandish (and later Italian) choral singers; and the fashion for things Italian in central Europe, which grew in the 17th century.

For singers who decide to aim at the Latin of a past time and place, the following sections give broad guidance, amplified in tables A-H (pages 22-43). Phonetic symbols are used in the ways defined in table Z at the end of the book.

England

The old Latin learnt by the Britons before the Germanic invasions did not directly affect English Latin, which began with missionaries from Ireland, Scotland and Rome in the sixth century; an Anglo-Saxon religious and literary culture developed, particularly under Alfred. After 1066 Latin was taught for 300 years by

Norman-French priests, and so medieval English Latin was not far from that on the continent.

Pronunciation from 1066 to 1400 is shown in Table A, 1-2. This is a period of long melismas, which we should sing well forward with the bony structure of the face, not in the throat. (Each professional choir must have come to an understanding about vowel quality as part of style; in no time or place should one assume uniformity throughout a country.)

In English, and in many other languages, each of the vowels is spoken with more than one quality. Nomenclature is confusing - the so-called **'short' and 'long' vowels** (written ă, ā, etc.) may have to be sung on a long note, even if they tend not to be thus spoken. The conventional 'short' and 'long' vowels, with their phonetic equivalents, are shown on the next page; note that three of them are now spoken as diphthongs.

I refer throughout to modern standard southern English, and I am conscious of northern, Scots and U.S. differences: in the U.S., for instance, ŏ is not usually [ɒ], nor is ū [ju]; Scots may say 'ar', 'or' as [ær] and [ɒr]. (Page L is for one's own comparisons.)

'Short'	'Long'
pat, [æ]	spate, [ei]; spark, [ɑ:]
pet, [ɛ]	peat, [i:]
pit, [I]	spite, [ai]
pot, [ɒ]	spoke, [ou]; sport, [ɔ:]
put, [U]; putt, [ʌ]	pool, [u:]; spume, [ju]

Tables A 1, 3 and 5 show that English vowels changed over the period in which Latin music has been written. (Apart from the mid-11th to mid-14th centuries, when Latin was taught in Anglo-Norman, Latin was read as if the words were English.) The long A, ā, having been a Germanic open back vowel, moved (perhaps with Norman influence) to a rather close forward one - [ɑ:], [a:], [æ:], [ɛ:], [e:] - and by the 18th century resembled the present [ei]. The long E moved from [ɛ:] through [e:] to the present tense [i:]. Long I moved from [i:] through [I:] and became a variety of diphthongs, [Ii], [əi], [ʌi], [ai]. These changes are shown in more detail in *SiL*, ch. 4 and 9.

The changes were rather rapid from 1400 to 1700, crossing the country from the north and east; they might also vary with social class, age and training. How this affected sung Latin is argued at length in *SiL*, 84f and 118-28: I conclude that trained choirs probably used purer vowels (surviving from earlier speech) than did most priests and monks, whose Latin resembled their current English speech.

The version at A 3 below is fairly conservative; chant by the clergy (other than the precentor) may have used more the advanced (i.e. later) vowels suggested in the notes.

Latin singing from the middle of the 16th century was limited to a few learned institutions and small illegal assemblies of Catholics. In the later seventeenth century there was some music for royal chapels, and Latin works have been written in the last century or so. My suggestion (elaborated in *SiL*, 194-9, 277-84) is that most but not all of the Latin music after 1650 was pronounced in the 'Old Style', the descendant of Tudor Latin which survives in the law and a few ancient colleges, where Latin is pronounced as in Standard English. Table A 3 provides some examples of how this works. Dictionaries originating many years back give examples of Latin words or phrases (particularly the *Oxford English Dictionary*).

France (*SiL*, ch. 10b, 11b).

Gallic Latin developed into French; when Latin itself was used, it followed the changing pronunciation of French. **Nasal vowels** before M or N began at different times (A and E quite early, and O, I and U between 1200 and 1400). The nasal consonant itself was sounded after the nasal vowel until the 16th century, when it gradually became absorbed in the vowel.

Throughout, the French habit is to lengthen end-syllables, especially at the ends of phrases; stress is absent or light, and what we and others regard as the normal 'tonic' accent is absent. Table B 3-4 gives guidance on the quality of vowels and consonants for the early medieval period, and B 5-6 for 1250-1650 in respect of Paris and central France. (I have assumed that the French Catholic Church was able to resist 16th-century pronunciation reforms for some time.)

B 3-4 has tentative suggestions for a Franco-Flemish Latin. Most French composers of 1250-1650 came from the north, some from Picardy (whose speech was close to that of the Walloons now within southern Belgium), others from Flanders and Brabant. It is worth attempting to find the sound of Latin with which Josquin, Lassus and the rest set out for European musical centres as the leading singers of their time. The Picards kept closer than the central French speech to the ancient Latin, where C was always [k]; the assibilation before E or I only got as far as [kj] or possibly [tʃ], instead of moving through [ts] to [s] as in French, Dutch or English. Nasality was common, and had its own rules.

B 7-8 gives the French Latin which remained in traditional use until very recently; it is appropriate for Fauré and Poulenc. It emerged from the muddle of partial reform in the sixteenth century, but it was some time before the French Church accepted it. So we have to guess what sort of Latin Lully, the Italian serving Louis XIV, used: probably French vowels and consonants, but (his music suggests) with Italian accentuation. The most recent generation of French composers may expect Roman Latin (with a French accent, as in *SiL* 290f).

Particularly since the sixteenth century, vowels may be different in open and in closed syllables. In French, words are divided so that syllables end with a vowel if possible, even if this means not sounding a final consonant; this vowel is lengthened and tensed, becoming a closer vowel of different quality. So *pa-ter* has an open ĕ, probably prolonged, giving [patɛ:r], but *lu-mi-ne* is [lymine].

It will be clear that historical French Latin is tricky. But learning it is musically rewarding: it is so different from our expectations.

Germany and central and northern Europe (*SiL*, ch. 10c, 11c, 11e).

Only the western part of the Germanic area was in the Roman empire, but in the seventh and eighth centuries Irish and English missionaries, later encouraged by Charlemagne, spread Christianity and thus Latin further east, and their relatively pure pronunciation does not seem to have changed much. As in medieval France and England, C before E or I is [ts], but G is always [g]. OE is sometimes pronounced as German ö (through a misunderstanding starting when humanist printers replaced *celi* by *coeli*): but [e:] is also sung, and is, I think, preferable for baroque and classical composers. Table C shows modern German Latin (opinions may differ: but singers in Germany will soon gather what is correct in their conductor's eyes).

Syllable division starts a new syllable with a consonant (*Chrĭs-te* compared with French *Chri-ste*). This affects vowel-quality; it is worth learning the practice in German speech.

Italy (*SiL*, ch. 10d, 11d, App. 8).

Table D summarises the Roman Style laid down in the English version of *Liber usualis*. This was prepared by the Benedictines of Solesmes and authorised by the Vatican in consequence of the reform of church life and music ordered by Pope Pius X in his decree *Motu proprio* (November 1903). Here the vowels are all open, as in Italian literary Latin (but not Italian itself). For music away from Rome, Florence and Bologna I think that Latin was closer to the vernacular, using close and open E and O. This applies especially to north-west Italy, where, in addition, the C and G before E or I has long been closer to French than to

Roman sounds.

A recent American booklet, *The Choral Director's Latin*, by Dr Ivan Trusler (Universities Press of America, 1987), gives full elementary instruction on singing Roman Latin, fairly close to *Liber usualis*. It has translations and phonetic transcriptions of several texts, with useful notes about their context. It does not however consider other pronunciations of Latin.

Iberian Renaissance music.

Table E gives pronunciation for **Spain**, and F for **Portugal**. This Spanish Latin is easier than modern Spanish because the medieval sibilants had not yet changed to their present values.

In general, **historical Latin pronunciation** can be deduced from the vernacular of the time if the results of any deliberate reforms are allowed for. Those who are not historical linguists will get some help by listening to native speakers reading Latin as if it were their own language, and using these (modern) sounds to colour my phonetic descriptions.

Table G summarises the '**compromise**' solution in *Choral Latin* (N.F.M.S , Francis House, Francis St., London SW1, 1960). This was worked out in the 1930s for leading choirs; it uses C and G (but not J) as in English, and Italian vowels. *Choral Latin* transcribes several texts into imitation English to indicate the compromise and the Italianate pronunciations.

There now follow Tables A to G, showing the **phonetic equivalent of key letters** in several styles of Latin. (There are important variants and qualifications in the corresponding sections of *SiL*, together with the sources and reasoning, and some historical background.) With the tables are corresponding specimen **phonetic texts**: see also *SiL*, 284-300.

For **phonetic signs** see Table Z (pages 46f).

Page 48 is left blank for readers'**preferred variants** and phonetic equivalents.

SiL gives fragmentary data for other countries and periods, on the following pages:

England before 1066, 112-5.

Scotland, Wales and Ireland, 135-41.

Eastern and northern Europe, 229f.

Venice and other Italian cities, 272-5.

North German and Dutch Latin, 300.

A 1

ENGLAND, 1066–1400

VOWELS (see *SiL*, 115f)
A. Ă, [a]; Ā varied from [ɑ:] to [ɛ:]: use
forward [a:].
AU, diphthong (not double vowel) [au].
E/AE/OE, [ɛ] when accented, but gradually moved
towards [e], especially when unaccented.
ER [ar] when accented, [ɛr] (not [ər]).
I, Y, [I] and [i:]; and see consonants.
O, [ɔ]; long vowel tending to [u:].
U, [U] and (in open syllable) [iu] or [y:].

LATIN TEXTS
Motet, Worcester, 14th c.
Alleluia psallat haec familia ... timpanis ... laetus coetus cum harmonia ...
Deo laudem et praeconia ...

Latin version of the 13th-c. round,
Sumer is icumen in
Perspice, christicola -/ que dignacio!
Celicus agricola,/ pro vitis vicio,
filio/ non parcens exposuit/ mortis exicio;
qui captivos semivivos/ a supplicio
vite donat/ et secum coronat/ in celi solio.

A 2

ENGLAND, 1066–1400

CONSONANTS (see *SiL*, 116f.)
C as [k], but before E,I etc. as [ts] until early 13th c., then [s]; **CC** as [kts], then [ks]; **Ecce**=[ɛktse,ɛkse].
CH, [kh], later [tʃ]; perhaps [ç] in **michi** etc.
G as [g], but before E,I etc. as [dʒ].
GN: [ŋgn], but sometimes [ŋn] or [n]. Not ñ.
I/J consonantal: as [dʒ]; so **cuius, eius.**
QU as [kw] but **quu** as [ku].
S as [s], but light [z] between vowels.
R rolled.
TI (not STI,XTI) +vowel: as [sI].
Z, [dz] until early 13th c., then [z].

PHONETIC TEXTS

Motet

[alelyja salat hɛk famIlla ... tImpanIs]
[lɛtUs kuetUs kUm harmunIa]
[dɛu laudem ɛt prekunIa]

Round

[parspItse khristIkula kwɛ dIŋgnatsIu]
[tsɛlIkUs agrIkula pru vitIs vItsIu]
[filiɔ nɔn partsɛnz=ekspɔzylt mɔrtIs egzitsIu]
[kwi kaptivu=semIvivus=a sUplItsIu]
[vite dɔnat=ɛt sekUm kurɔnat In tsɛlI sɔlIu]

A 3

ENGLAND, 1400–1650

VOWELS (for **polyphony and choral chant**: see discussion in *SiL*, 120–8, 292–5)
A: Ă as forward [a], Ā as [æ:].
AU, [au].
E,AE,OE: [ɛ], [e:]; unaccented, [i,I].
I,Y: Ĭ, [I], Ī as in 'machine'.
IE in **Kyrie** usually [i].
O, as [ɔ,ɔ:]
U: Ŭ, [U]; Ū, [Y:] but [u:] after R or J.
For **chant** sung by priests and monks, and in **carols** etc., use an 'advanced' pronunciation:
A=[æ,ɛ:].
E=[ɛ,i:].
I=[I,əi].
O=[ɔ,o:].
U=[U,ju:].

LATIN TEXT
Priest: Credo in unum Deum
Choir: patrem omnipotentem,
factorem c(a)eli et terr(a)e, visibilium omnium
et invisibilium, et in unum Dominum
Iesum Christum, Filium Dei unigenitum
et ex Patre natum ante omnia s(a)ecula
Deum de Deo, Lumen de lumine, Deum verum de
Deo vero. Genitum, non factum, consubstantialem
Patri, per quem omnia facta sunt. [etc.]

A 4

ENGLAND, 1400-1650

CONSONANTS (see *SiL*, 129-32)
Before **e,ae,oe,i**:
C,SC=[s].
CC=[ks]; **ecce**=[ɛksi].
CH=[tʃ]; **cherubim** etc. have [k].
G is usually [dʒ] but [g] in **gimel**.
Otherwise **C,CH,K**=[k]; **G**=[g].
GN=[ŋgn].
H (initial) light, but **Hierusalem** etc. have [dʒ]; **mihi,nihil** have [tʃ] or [ç].
I/J=[dʒ]: **Iesu, cujus. ejus, eia** have [e:dʒ-].
QU, [kw] but **quo,quum** as [ko,kUm].
R trilled.
S=[s] as initial, and often final, consonant; light [z] if between vowels.
-TIA,TIO, with [si-], but in 17th c. [ʃi] or [ʃ].

PHONETIC TEXT
Priest: [kri:do In junəm di:əm]
Choir: [pæ:trɛm ɔmnIpɔtɛntɛm
faktɔrɛm seli ɛ=tɛre vizibl:liUm ɔmniUm
ɛt InVIzibl:liUm ɛt In YnUm dɔmInUm
dʒezUm krIstUm fIliUm dei YnidʒɛnitUm
ɛt ɛks pæ:tre næ:tUm ante ɔmnia sekYla
deUm de deɔ lYmɛn de lymIne deUm vɛrUm de
deɔ vɛrɔ dʒɛnitUm nɔn faktUm kɔnsUb-
stansialɛm patri pɛr kwɛm ɔmnia fakta sUnt]

A 5

ENGLAND, from 1650

VOWELS (see *SiL*, 194-9, 277-82)
A: Ă=[æ], Ā=[ɛ:], then [e:]; later [ei].
E/AE/OE, [ɛ,i:]
I/Y, [I,ai].
O, [ɒ,ow].
U, [U], later [ʌ]; [ju:].

LATIN TEXT: Anthem, H. Purcell, late 17th c.
Jehova, quam multi sunt hostes mei!
...insurgunt contra me!...dicunt de anima mea, non est ulla salus isti in Deo plane.
At Tu, Jehova, clypeus es circa me: Gloria mea et extollens caput meum. Voce mea ad Jehovam clamanti respondit mihi e monte sanctitatis suæ maxime. Ego cubui et dormivi, ego expergefeci me, quia Jehova sustentat me.
Non timebo a myriadibus populi quas circum disposuerint metatores contra me. Surge Jehova, fac salvum me Deus mi. Qui percussisti omnes inimicos meos maxillam, dentes improborum confregisti. Jehova est salus, super populum tuum sit benedictio tua maxime.

Carol, de Pearsall, 1837: In dulci jubilo ... Matris in gremio ... O Jesu parvule ... trahe me post te ... O Patris caritas ... O nati lenitas ... per ... cœlorum gaudia ... ubi ... Regis curia ...

A 6

ENGLAND, from 1650

CONSONANTS (see *SiL*, 277-82)
C,CC,CH,G,S: as in A4.
GN, [gn].
H, [h].
I/J, [dʒ].
QU, [kw].
-TIA,-TIO, with [ʃi] or [ʃ].

PHONETIC TEXTS
[dʒIhovə kwam mUltai sUnt hɔstiz miai ... InsUrgUnt kɔntra mi ... daikUnt de ænImə mie ... nɔn ɛst Ula sɛilUs Istai In deo plɛ:ni
æt tju dʒIhova kIIpiUs ɛst sərkə mi glɔriə mie ɛt ɛkstɔlɛnz kapUt miUm vosi mie æ=dʒIhovəm kləmæntai rIspɔndIt maihai i mɔnti sæŋktItɛ:tIs sjui mæksImi ɛgo kjubjul ɛt dɔrmaivl ɛgo ɛkspərdʒifisl mi kwaiə dʒIhovə sUstɛntæt mi nɔn tImibo e mIrIɛ:dIməs pɔpjulai kwæs sərkəm dIspɔzjuirInt mɛtatɔriz kɔntrə mi sə:rdʒi dʒI-hovə fæk salvəm mi diəs mai kwai pərkjusIstai ɔmniz InImaikɔs miɔs mæksIlæm dɛntiz Improb-ɔrəm kɔnfrIdʒIstai dʒIhova ɛst sɛ:lUs sjupər pɔpjuləm tjuəm sIt bɛnIdIkʃio tjuə mæksImi]

[In dʌlsI dʒu:bIlow ... meitrIs In gri:miow ... ow dʒizju parvjuli ... treihi mi powst ti ... ow pætrIs kɛərItæs ... ow neitai li:nitæs ... pə: ... silɔrəm gɔ:dli ... jubi ... ridʒIs kjurieil]

B 1

FRANCE, to 1250

VOWELS (see *SiL*, 145f)
A, forward [a].
AM,AN, forward [ãm,ãn].
E/AE/OE, if accented, [e]; if not, [ə] or mute.
EM, EN, [ɛm,ɛn] to 1050, then [ãm,ãn].
ER, [ar].
I, [i]; **[IN]**, [in].
O, [ɔ] to 1200, then [o].
OM,ON, [om] ('ome'), [on].
U, [y], but:
UM,UN, [ym,yn], or [om,on].

LATIN TEXT (13th c. clausulae)
Hec dies quem fecit Dominus:
exsultemus et laetemur in ea.
Confitemini Domino quoniam bonus:
In seculum misericordia ejus.

FRANCE, to 1250

CONSONANTS (see *SiL*, 147)
Before E,I:
C,SC, [ts].
CC, [ks].
G, [dʒ], English 'g'.
H, generally mute except Norman and Picard.
I/J consonantal, [dʒ].
M,N, see opposite.
QU, [k] (but Norman [kw] except in **quum**).
S, [s] at start of syllable but [z] between vowels, and at end of words.
-TIA,-TIO, with [ts].
X, usually [z].
Z, [dz].
GROUPS: many consonants elided, e.g.
ANT/ANCT/EMPT = [ãt].

PHONETIC TEXT
[ek diez kãm fetsi=dɔminyz]
[ezultemyz=e letemyr in=ea]
[konfitemini dɔmino kɔniãm bɔnyz]
[in secylym mizərikɔrdia=edʒyz]

B 3

FRANCO-FLEMISH (tentative Picard version)

VOWELS (see 14f and *SiL*, 155f)
A, [a], but **AM**=[ãm]; **AN**=[ã] ([ãn] before vowel).
AU, [au].
E/AE/OE, [e] in open syll., [ɛ] in a closed: but
EM,EN as [ɛ̃m,ɛ̃n], not developing to modern [ɑ̃].
ER tended to [ar].
I,Y as [i]. However:
IM,IN nasalised, post-1500, to [ĩ] or [ẽ] or
[eim,ein] (not to Fr. [ɛ̃]).
O: ō was [o], moving to [u] by 16th c.; ŏ, [ɔ].
OM,ON gradually became [ũm,ũn].
U, as [Y] (not as tense as Fr. [y]), but:
UM,UN were [Ỹm,Ỹn] from c.1400, gradually
becoming [œ̃m,œ̃n], or [ɛ̃m,ɛ̃n]; in 17th c. [œ̃].
A Picard vowel was not nasalised if there
was a nasal vowel later in the word.
AM/AN and probably EM/EN, even followed by a
vowel, were nasal before an unaccented ending.

LATIN TEXT (Josquin)
Ave Maria, gratia plena, Dominus tecum. ...
Ave vera virginitas, immaculata castitas,
cujus purificatio nostra fuit purgatio.
Ave preclara omnibus angelicis virtutibus,
cujus fuit assumptio nostra glorificatio.
O mater Dei, memento mei. Amen

B 4

FRANCO-FLEMISH (tentative Picard version)

CONSONANTS (see *SiL*, 157f)
C before a,o,u, as [k]. Before E,I, [kj] or [tʃ].
CH mainly [k].
G, [g] but before e,i, as [ʒ].
GN, [gn] or [xn].
H, mute (but strong in **mihi**, **nihil**, **Hier**–).
I/J consonantal, as [ʒ].
QU, probably [k] before all vowels.
R: weakening but still [r], not uvular.
S: [z] between vowels and possibly at end of word; **SC** in **descendo** etc. as [k]: [dekɛ̃ndo].
ST: s becomes gh, so **est** as [ɛxt].
-TIA,-TIO,-TIONE were [tʃia,zio,ziʊne].
X; **XC** before E,I; **Z**: probably [z].
Consonantal groups perhaps somewhat elided.

PHONETIC TEXT
[ave maria gratʃia plena dʊminYx=tekYm]
[ave vara virʒinitaz imakYlata kaxtitaz]
[kYʒYz pYrifikazio nɔxtra fYit pYrgazio]
[ave preklara ɔ̃nibYz ãʒelikjiz virrtYtibYz]
[kYʒy=fYit asỸmzio nɔxtra glɔrifikazio]
[o matɛr dei memɛ̃nto mei amɛ̃n]

B 5

FRANCE, 1250-1650, unreformed

VOWELS (see 7f, 14; *SiL* 160-3)
A, forward [a].
AM,AN, [ãm,ãn] to 1500, then [ã],
but [am],[an] before C,Q,G,P.
AU, [au] to 1300, [ao] 1300-1500, then [o].
E/AE/OE, in open syllable [e], not very close;
in closed syllable, [ɛ]. But:
EM,EN, [ãm],[ãn] to 1550, then forward [ã].
ER if accented, [ar] (terra='tara').
I, [i], but:
IM,IN, [ĩm,ĩn]; post-1500 also [in]/[im], or [ɛ̃].
O, [o], later [u], but:
OM,ON gradually nasalised by 14th c. in central
France to [õ],[ɔ̃] plus consonant; post-1500,
[ɔ̃] alone. In provinces, [ũm,ũn] throughout.
U, [y]: but **UM,UN** from 1400-1550 [ỹm,ỹn];
post-1550, [õ], or else as Fr. 'un'.

LATIN TEXT (Hart's *An Orthography*, 1569)
Pater noster qui es in celis,
sanctificetur nomen tuum, adveniat nomen tuum,
fiat voluntas tua sicut in celo et in terra:
panem nostrum quotianum da nobis hodie,
et dimite nobis debita nostra,
sicut et nos dimitimus debitoribus nostris:
et ne nos dimitimus in temptationem:
sed libera nos a malo.

FRANCE, 1250–1650, unreformed

CONSONANTS (see 7f, 15; *SiL*, 163-5)
Before E,I:
  C,SC, CC, [s].
  CH, [ʃ] but otherwise [k].
  G,I/J, [ʒ] (French 'g').
GN, normally [n].
H in mihi, nihil, [ʃ]; in **Hier–usalem** etc., [ʒ]; otherwise mute.
QU, [k].
R, trilled; **RR,** doubled.
S, [s] at start of syllable but [z] between vowels, and at end of words.
TIA,TIO, [sia],[sio].
X; **CT** in resurrectio, [z]; **EX** as Fr. 'euz'.
Z, normally [z].
ELISION: consonants in groups and at ends of words dropped readily; **et, est,** could be [e,ɛ].

PHONETIC TEXT: Hart's transcription, *SiL*, 90
[pa:tɛr nɔstɛr kiɛz in seli:z]
[sãntifsetyr nomɛn tyym atveniat rejnym tyym]
[fiat volynta:z tya sikyt in selo e in ta:ra]
[panem nostrym kotidianym da nobi:z odi:e]
[e dimi:te nobi: debi:ta nostra]
[sikyt et noz dimi:timyz debitɔribyz nostri:z]
[et ne noz indyka:z in tɛntasionɛm]
[set libɛranoz a malo amãn]

B 7

FRANCE, from 1650 ('traditional')

VOWELS (see 15; *SiL* 206-8, 292, 296f)

A, forward [a], but **AM,AN** = [am,an] (if a non-nasal consonant follows, [ɑ̃] + consonants).
AU, [o], not [au].
E,AE,OE, [e] (open syllable); closed, usually [ɛ].
EM,EN, [ɑ̃], but by 1800 [ɛm,ɛn].
EMP, ENT, [ɛ̃mp,ɛ̃nt] (others comparably)
EU. Normally as Fr. 'eu', [ø].
I, Y, [i]; **IM,IN**, [ɛ̃], but may be [im,in] or (mid-18th c.) [ĩm,ĩn].
O, [ɔ]; often [o] in open syllable.
OM,ON [ɔ̃] + consonant if non-nasal; [ɔ] if before two nasal consonants; **non** = [nɔn].
U before non-nasal consonant, [y].
UM, UN, [om,on], to 1800, then close to [ɒm,ɒn].
UNC, [œ̃t]; **UNT**, [õt] to 1800, then [ɔ̃t].

LATIN TEXT (Charpentier, d.1704)
Te Deum laudamus, Te Dominum confitemur
Te æternum Patrem omnis terra veneratur
Tibi omnes Angeli/ cœli et universæ potestates
Tibi Cherubim et Seraphim incessabili voce
proclamant Sanctus Dominus Deus Sabaoth.
Pleni sunt cœli et terra majestatis gloriæ tuæ.
[etc.]

B 8

FRANCE, from 1650 (traditional)

CONSONANTS (see 15; *SiL*, 209f, 291, 296f)
Before E,AE,OE,I,Y:
 C,SC, [s].
 CC, [s] ([ks] from 1700).
 CH, usually [k] but [ʃ] might still be used.
 G, consonantal I/J, [ʒ] (Fr. 'g').
GN, ñ in most words, but [gn] in **agnus, dignus**.
H, generally mute.
QU: **qua**, [kwa]; **que, quae**, [kẅe]; **qui**, [kẅi]; **quo**, [ko]; **quum**, [kom]; **equus**, [ekys].
S, [s] but [z] between vowels (ignoring word-boundaries); [s] in compounds like **desuper**.
S,T: not dropped at ends of words (**et,est** are [et,ɛst]).
TI + vowel, [si].
X,XC, [ks] but [gs] before a vowel.
Z, [z].

PHONETIC TEXT
[te deom lodamys te dɔminom kɔ̃nfitemyr]
[te etɛrnom patrãm=ɔnis tɛra veneratyr]
[tibi ɔnez=ɑ̃nʒeli/ seli et=ynivɛrse pɔtɛstates]
[tibi kerybĩm et serfĩm ĩnsesabile vose]
[proklamɑ̃nt sɑ̃ntyz=dominys=dey=sabaɔt]
[pleni sɔ̃n=seli=e=tɛra maʒɛstatiz=glorie tye]

C 1

GERMANY, modern standard

VOWELS (see 16f, especially on open and closed syllables; *SiL*, 217-9)
A, [a,a:]; **Amen**, [a:mɛn].
AU, [ao] (for Bach's time see *SiL*).
AE: now [ɛ,ɛ:]; earlier, as E. See OE.
E: stressed, [ɛ,e:]; unstressed, **light** [ɛ,e].
EU: as in German, [ɔy]: but **Deus**=[de:Us].
I: open stressed syllable, [i:]; closed, or unstressed, [I]; final, [i].
-**IS**=[Is] but **his**=[hi:s].
O: open stressed syllable, [o:] (but [ɔ] in **Dominus, homines, oriens**); final, [o]; in closed syllables, [ɔ] (endings tend to [ɒ]).
OE: **coelum/caelum, poeni** usually as German 'oe', [ø:]: sometimes [ɛ:].
U: [U,u:]; -**UM**,-**US** [Um,Us].
Y: now [Y,y:] (earlier, as I).
GLOTTAL STOP before initial vowel: in excelsis.
NO LIAISON as in French, etc.

LATIN TEXT: from Ordinary of the Mass
Kyrie eleison, Christe eleison.
Sanctus Dominus Deus Sabaoth,
pleni sunt coeli gloria tua.
Hosanna in excelsis.
Benedictus qui venit in nomine Domini.
Agnus Dei, qui tollis peccata mundi,
miserere nobis/ dona nobis pacem.

Update Sept, 1990

GERMANY, modern standard

CONSONANTS (and see *SiL* 170, 219-21)
B,D as final consonants are [p,t].
C=[k]: but [ts] before E,I,AE,OE,Y.
CC=[k]: but [kts] before E etc.; ecce=[ɛktse].
CH as initial, usually [k]. After A (**Rachel**), [x];
after E,I or a consonant (**Michael**), as [ç].
G is now always [g]; **GN**=[gn] (earlier, [ŋn]).
H=[h].
I/J consonantal, now as [j].
QU,GU,SU (+ vowel): the U is a quick [v].
R is rolled, except in weak endings (-**ER** etc.)
S: initial, [s] but sometimes [z] in the north;
final, [s]; between vowels, [z]; [s] in **eleison**.
SC before E,I, [sts]; **SCA**, [ska]; **SP,ST**, [sp,st].
-**TIA**,-**TIO**, generally with [tsi].
XC before E, [ksts].
Z=[ts].
DOUBLED CONSONANTS are pronounced single.

PHONETIC TEXT
[ky:rie elɛisɔn krIste elɛisɔn]
[saŋktUs dɔmInUs de:Us sa:baɔt]
[ple:ni sUnt tsø:li ɛ=tɛra glo:ria tu:a]
[hosana In ɛkstsɛlsIs] (or [hoza:na])
[benedIktUs kvi ve:nIt In no:minɛ dɔmIni]
[a:gnUs de:i kvi tɔlIs pɛka:ta mUndi]
[misɛre:re no:bIs do:na no:bIs pa:tsɛm]

D 1

ITALY, Roman Style

VOWELS (see *SiL*, 226f)
A=[a,a:].
E=[ɛ,ɛ:].
I,Y=[i,i:].
O=[ɔ,ɔ:].
U=[u,u:].

LATIN TEXT (Palestrina)
Exultate Deo adjutori nostro,
jubilate Deo Jacob!
Sumite psalmum et date tympanum,
psalterium jucundum cum cythara!
Buccinate in neomenia tuba,
insigni die solemnitatis vestræ!

ITALY, Roman Style

CONSONANTS (see *SiL*, 227f)
Before E,I, etc.:
  C=[tʃ].
  CC=[ttʃ] (**ecce**).
  G=[dʒ] (**genitum**).
Otherwise C=[K], G=[g].
CH=[k].
GN is a prolonged ñ.
H is mute, but [k] in **mihi, nihil.**
I/J consonantal=[j].
QU=[kw].
R is rolled.
S=[s] but slight [z] between vowels.
TH=[t].
TI+vowel=[tsi-], including *Pontio*
X=[ks], or [gs] between vowels.
Z=[dz].
DOUBLED CONSONANTS are clearly sounded.

PHONETIC TEXT
[ɛgsultatɛ dɛɔ adjutɔri nɔstrɔ]
[jubilatɛ dɛɔ jakɔb]
[sumitɛ salmum ɛt datɛ timpanum]
[saltɛrium jukundum kum tʃitara]
[buttʃinate in nɛɔmɛmia tuba]
[insiñɛ diɛ sɔlɛmnitatis vɛstrɛ]

E 1

RENAISSANCE SPAIN

VOWELS (see *SiL*, 177)
A=[a].
E=[e] generally, but [ɛ] if next to RR, and in syllables closed other than by d,m,n,s,z.
I=[i].
O is [o] in an open syllable, [ɒ] in a closed.
U=[u].

LATIN TEXT (Guerrero)
Pastores loquebantur ad invicem transeamus
usque Bethlem et videamus hoc verbum
quod factum est, quod fecit Dominus
et ostendit nobis, et venerunt festinantes,
et invenerunt Mariam, et Joseph,
et infantem positum in praesepio. Alleluia.
Videntes autem cognoverunt de verbo
quod dictum erat illis de puero hoc
Et omnes qui audierunt mirati sunt: et de his
quae dicta erant a pastoribus ipsos.
Maria autem conservabat omnia verba haec,
conferens in corde suo. Alleluia.

RENAISSANCE SPAIN

CONSONANTS (*SiL*, 177-9)

C, Ç, SC before E,I etc. as [ts] with the [t] faint; **ecce** probably [ɛktse].
G=[g] but [ʒ] before E,I.
GN as ñ, or as [gn] with the [g] light.
H silent, even in **mihi, nihil**.
I/J consonantal = [ʒ].
QUA- =[kwa]; before other vowels QU = [k].
RR is strongly trilled.
TI + vowel, [tsi] or (reformed) [ti].
V, as for B (which is non-explosive).
X, [ks] or [ss]; [ʃ] between vowels (**resurrexit**).
Z. [dz] or [tz].

PHONETIC TEXT

[pastores lokebantur ad invitsem transeamus]
[uske bɛtlem ɛt videamus ɒk bɛrbum]
[kɒd faktum ɛst kɒd fetsit dominus]
[ɛt ɒstendit nobis ɛt benerunt fɛstinantes]
[ɛt invenerunt mariam ɛt ʒozɛf]
[ɛt infantem pozitum in prezepio aleluja]
[bidɛntes autem koñoverunt de bɛrbo]
[kɒ=diktum erat ilis de puero ɒk]
[ɛt omnes ki audierunt mirati sunt ɛt de is]
[ke dikta erant a pastoribus ipsos]
[maria autem konserbabat omnia bɛrba ɛk]
[konferens in kɒrde suo aleluja]

F 1

RENAISSANCE PORTUGAL
VOWELS (see *SiL*, 181)
Except before M or N:
A, as [a], but as [ə] in 'sofa' if unstressed.
E, as [ɛ] if stressed. Otherwise [e], [i].
I = [i].
O. [ɔ] if stressed; final -O tends to [u].
U = [u].
NASAL VOWELS: M/N at end of word, or before a consonant, nasalised the preceding vowel;
-AM/AN,-EM/EN,-UM then become [ã],[ɛ̃],[ũ] (Amen is [amɛ̃]).

-ANT,-ENT,-UNT=[ãt],[ɛ̃t],[ũt]; before MM,MN,NN the vowel is slighly nasal.

A **medial** vowel followed by M,N + consonant is nasalised, and [m,n] is weakened (Redemptor).

LATIN TEXT (Duarte Lobo)
Requiem aeternam dona nobis Domine:
et lux perpetua luceat eis.
Te decet hymnus Deus in Sion
et tibi reddetur votum in Jerusalem:
exaudi orationem meam,
ad te omnis caro veniet.

Kyrie eleison. Christe eleison.

F 2

RENAISSANCE PORTUGAL

CONSONANTS (see *SiL*, 181f)
Before E,I, etc.:
  C,CC=[s]; **ecce**=[ɛse].
  G=[ʒ].
Otherwise C=[k], G=[g].
CH=[k].
GN=[gn].
H mute, but [ʃ] or [k] in **mihi, nihil.**
I/J consonantal, as [ʒ].
NC, NG as [ŋk], [ŋg].
QU is [kw] before A,O,U; [k] before E,I.
R strongly trilled in initials, ends of
  syllables, and in RR,SR).
S as [s], but [z] between vowels.
X. Probably [ks] but [gs] before a vowel.
Z=[z].

PHONETIC TEXT
[rɛkiɛ̃m=etɛrnã dona nɔbis dɔmini]
[ɛt luks perpɛtua luseat ɛis]
[te dɛset ĩmnus dɛus in siõn]
[ɛt tibi redɛtur vɔtũm in ʒerusalẽm]
[egsaudi orasiɔnẽ=mɛãm]
[a=tɛ ɔ̃mnis karo vɛniet]

[kirielɛizõn kristelɛizõn]

G 1

'COMPROMISE' (as in *Choral Latin*)

VOWELS (see *Choral Latin*, 2f; *SiL*, 356)
A, 'ah', meaning [a,a:] rather than [æ].
E: 'e' or 'air', [ɛ,ɛ:]; 'ay', [e,e:].
I: ĭ is 'i', [ɪ]; ī is 'ee', [i:].
O: ŏ is 'o', [ɒ] or [ɔ]; ō is 'oh', [o,o:].
U, always 'oo', [u,u:].

TEXT in imitative English (*Choral Latin*, 11f)
Stahbaht Mahtair dolorohsa
Yooxta croosem lahcrimohsa,
Doom pendaybaht Feeliooce.
Cooyooce ahnimahm jementem,
Contreestahtahm et dolentem,
Pairtrahnseevit glahdiooce.
O quahm treestis et ahfleecta
Fooit illa benedicta
Mahtair Oonijenitee;
Quay moraybaht et dolaybaht
Peea Mahtair, doom veedaybaht
Nahtee paynahce inclitee.
Queece est ohmo quee non flairet
Mahtrem Creestee see vidairet
In tahnto soopleesio?
Queece non posset contreestahree
Creestee Mahtrem contemplahree
Dohlentem coom Feelio? [etc.]

G 2

'COMPROMISE' (as in *Choral Latin*)

CONSONANTS are [mostly] as in English. But H is treated as silent, J as if it was Y, and -TIO as [tio] rather than [sio], [ʃio] or [ʃo].

Conductors can of course set up their own compromises: see *SiL*, 356, for one suggestion.

I attempt below a phonetic interpretation, without endorsing details of the pronunciation.

PHONETIC TEXT following version on p. 44

[stabat matɛr dɔlɔrosa]
[juksta krusɛm lakrɪmosa]
[dum pɛndebat filɪus]
[kujus animam dʒɛmɛntɛm]
kɒntristatam ɛt dɔlɛntɛm]
[pɛrtransivɪt gladius]
[o kwam tristɪs ɛt aflikta]
[fuit ɪla bɛnɛdɪkta]
[matɛr unɪdʒɛniti]
[kwe mɔrebat ɛt dɔlebat]
[pia matɛr dum videbat]
[nati penas ɪnklɪti]
[kwis ɛst omɔ kwi nɒn flɛrɛt]
[matrɛm kristi si vɪdɛrɛt]
[ɪn tantɔ suplisɪɔ]
[kwis nɒn pɒsɛt kɒntristari]
[kristi matrɛm kɒntɛmplari]
[dɔlɛntɛm kum filɪɔ]

Z 1

PHONETIC SIGNS (using British English)

[ ] indicates a **phonetic** symbol; for values see below. A colon, e.g. [a:], means that the sound [a] is **prolonged**.

Open vowels have jaw and tongue low; **close** vowels have tongue closer to the palate.

In **back** vowels the tongue is arched at the back, and in **front** vowels at the front. **Tense/lax** refers to muscles of the mouth.

VOWELS

[ɑ] - open back ā: Fr.*pas*

[a] - clear open forward a: It.*mama mia*

[æ] - forward close ă: *mat*.

[e] - close e: Fr.*été*, Ger.*See*.

[ɛ] - open ĕ: *met*.

[I] - open ĭ: *sit*; I use **[I:]** for the vowel in *machine*, with lips forward.

[i] - close tense vowel: Fr.*si*.

[o] - rounded close o: *poet*, Fr.*sauter*.

[ɔ] - more open: Ger.*Gott*; [ɔ:], *ought*.

[ɒ] - open English ŏ: *not* (U.S. differs).

[u] - lips closely rounded, Fr.*foule*; [u:], *loot*.

[U] - S. English *look*; N. English ŭ.

[ʌ] - modern S. English ŭ: *luck*.

[y] - close rounded forward: Fr.*volume*.

[Y] - less forward: Ger. *Küche*.

PHONETIC SIGNS - contd.

[ə] - weak central vowels: *father, about, gallop*; Fr.*petit*.
[ø:] - as in Ger. *böse*.

NASAL VOWELS

A tilde, e.g. [ã], makes [a] **nasal**.

Familiar French nasal vowels are [ɛ̃] in *faim, vin*; [ɑ̃] in *blanc*; [ɔ̃] in *patron*; [œ̃] in *un*.

Unfamiliar vowels occur in French and Portuguese Latin: [ã] (a forward vowel), [ẽ], [ĩ], [õ], [ũ], [Ỹ], [ỹ]. To produce these, nasalise with lips and tongue as for each oral vowel.

SEMIVOWELS (glides)
[j] - quick [I]: *yet, you*.
[w], **[ẅ]** - quick [u], [y].

CONSONANTS (where not obvious)
[g] - *got, get*.
[ŋ] - as in Std. Eng. *sing*.
[ʃ] - English *sh*, modern French *ch*.
[θ] - th in *theta, thing*
[ʒ] - leisure, Fr.*j'ai*.
[x] - Scots *loch*, Ger.*ach*.
[z] - *zeal*.

I have used **ñ** (not an orthodox phonetic character) for the sound in (Spanish) *mañana*.

NOTES AND VARIATIONS